THE CHRIST-CENTERED DIY COACHING MANUAL FOR WOMEN

BARBARA A. PERRY

Elohim's Estate Class Session Material
by Barbara A. Perry

Copyright © 2021 Barbara A. Perry

ALL RIGHTS RESERVED

ISBN: 978-0-9960442-7-1

NO PART OF THIS BOOK MAY BE REPRODUCED IN ANY FORM, BY PHOTOCOPING OR BY ANY ELECTRONIC OR MECHANICAL MEANS, INCLUDING INFORMATION STORAGE OR RETRIEVAL SYSTEMS, WITHOUT PERMISSION IN WRITING FROM THE COPYRIGHT OWNER/AUTHOR.

Printed in the U.S.A.

GARDEN 33 PUBLISHER

COURSE MATERIAL CONTENT

		Page Number
1.	Introduction To Session Material.....................................	5
2.	Ambassador's Attitude..	6
3.	Class Schedule (Suggested)	8
4.	How To Do Class Sessions...	10
5.	Miracle – Water made wine in Cana	16
6.	Miracle – Creation of the World...................................	18
7.	Miracle – 10 Plagues in Egypt.....................................	20
8.	Miracle – Draught of Fishes...	22
9.	Miracle – Two Demoniac Cured...................................	26
10.	Miracle – Naaman Cured of Leprosy............................	29
11.	Miracle – Increase of the Widow's Oil..........................	34
12.	Miracle – Elisha Prophesies Plenty in Samaria...............	36
13.	A study of II Peter 1: 3 – 11...	43
14.	Some Groundwork Information on Prayer.....................	49
15.	The Similarity Between Jabez Prayer and the Lord's Prayer..........	51
16.	Seeing or Revealing Me List..	52
17.	Mentor's Speech...	53
18.	Class Exit Survey...	54

TO THE KING OF KINGS AND LORD OF LORDS
To all glory belongs!

"This Book of the Law shall not depart from your mouth, but you shall meditate in it day and night, that you may observe to do according to all that is written in it. For then you will make your way prosperous, and then you will have good success." Joshua 1:8 NKJV

INTRODUCTION TO THE MANUAL

In this manual are 12 Sessions centered on –

- Character
- Miracles
- Life/self discovery
- The Mind
- Goals Setting
- Personal hindrances
- Prayer : Ground Work Instruction

Also includes:

- Meditation Exercises from Biblical Events/Accounts
- Bible Chapter Presentation (Public Speaking)
- An Ambassador's Attitude to Adopt

Some objectives of the lessons are to help you:
- Awaken your inner-self
- Rebuild your inner-self
- Advance your inner-self
- Recover you
- Discover or rediscover something new about you
- Restore hope
- Awaken imagination
- Envision again
- Get a vision

Hope you enjoy the journey to the new you!

Barbara A. Perry, Kingdom Priest

AMBASSADOR'S ATTITUDE
BE KINGDOM MINDED

∞∞∞∞∞∞∞∞∞∞∞∞∞∞∞∞∞∞∞∞∞∞∞

A - I am artistic and wonderfully designed!

M - I am a miracle. I'm marvelous. Like the Earth - I multiply!

B - I am as bold and empowering as a Lioness!

A - I am as amazing as an ocean wave - I rise high!

S - Like the sunrise, I refuse to be restrained!

S - I am strong and as successful as a songbird!

A - Like an eagle, I aspire to new heights!

D - I am as diligent as an ant - building life!

O - I am as optimism as a turtle - remaining hopeful in the dark!

R - I am a refresher like water - releasing life!

∞∞∞∞∞∞∞∞∞∞∞∞∞∞∞∞∞∞∞∞∞∞∞∞

I am Ambassador Barbara A. Perry, Kingdom Priest

Class Schedule (Suggested)

Note: You can use this schedule as a guide for your personal sessions or draft your own. It can also be used for a small group setting (No charge to students)!

- Opening Prayer
- Session Lesson in How to do the session
- Bible chapter presentation
- Home Work Review
- Character Development/Growth In Christ
    - *2nd Peter 1:1 – 14
    - *Gal. 5:22; *Col.3:12
- Supernatural/Miracle Events Worksheets
- Open questions and sharing [as time permits]

++

1. Assign Homework
2. Bible chapter reading: Have student pluck a book and read a chapter or event from it and be prepared to tell (public speaking) what they received from it at the next session.

*Note: Write the names of the books of the Bible on pieces of paper, put in a box or bag and have 1 or 2 students (according to class management time) pluck from the bag and be prepared to share with class on next meeting day.

-       Closing Prayer

Regarding Miracle Lessons: There are 8 miracle lessons. You should start using them in the 2nd Session meeting. Do not give students the miracle lessons upfront. Give them a lesson in each session in the listed order when you come to that point in "How To Do The Class Sessions".

****

The Below material is in the Welcome Package. Download it from website:
barbaraperry.wixsite.com/elohimestatemlc

Look over material and use your judgment on when and if to add them. Please remember class time management:

- Tolerations
- Brain Storm Worksheet
- 7 Powerful Questions to Help You Find Life Purpose
- 37 Coaching Questions to Liberate Clients

Please download the Welcome Package and review it to get a feel for how you want to arrange your personal study sessions time, if the above class schedule does not suit you.

Note: Print the Seeing Or Revealing Me Chart in <u>Landscape Mode!</u>

How To Do The Class Sessions
&
Homework Assignment by Sessions

> Please keep in mind that each individual class time and session may flow differently, so you will need to make any adjustments as necessary.

Please see page 8. There's a note about the Miracle Lessons.

****

Date : _____

SESSION 1 [Review Welcome Package]

- Wheel of Life
- S.M.A.R.T Goal
- Character Development [Growth In Christ sheet with list of virtues, etc. Have them read verses and write definition. Inform them that they will be completing a worksheet on II Peter 1:1 – 14 in Session 8 1st – 5 questions from 25 Powerful Pondering Questions

> Introduce Mentee to these; then start working on these as time permits. Complete the rest for homework.

- Bible presentations (selected students)_____
  Homework adjustment, if any:_____
  _____
  _____

Date : _____

SESSION 2

- Bible presentations
- Review homework from session 1
- Miracle – Water made Wine in Cana

- 2nd – 5 questions from 25 Powerful Pondering Questions
- Seeing or Revealing Me Chart (Character: **Adam**)

> Limited time for reviewing home-work so time will be given to Miracles. Start working on these, if time permits. Complete the rest for homework.

- Bible presentations (selected students)_____
  Homework adjustment, if any:_____
  _____
  _____

Date : _____

SESSION 3

- Bible presentations
- Review homework from session 2
- Miracle – Creation of the World

- S.M.A.R.T Goals Sheet, Brain Storm, or Tolerations
- Seeing or Revealing Me Chart
  (Character: **Eve**)

> Limited time for reviewing home-work so time will be given to Miracles. Start working on these, if time permits. Complete the rest for homework.

- Bible presentations (selected students) _____
  Homework adjustment, if any: _____
  _____
  _____

Date : _____

SESSION 4

- Bible Presentation
- Review homework from session 3
- Miracle -10 Plagues in Egypt

- 3rd – 5 questions from 25 Powerful Pondering Questions
- Seeing or Revealing Me Chart (Character: **Cain**)

> Limited time for reviewing home-work so time will be given to Miracles. Start working on these, if time permits. Complete the rest for homework.

- Bible presentations (selected students) _____
  Homework adjustment, if any: _____
  _____
  _____

Date : _____

SESSION 5

- Bible presentations
- Review homework from session 4
- Miracle – Draught of Fishes

- 4th – 5 questions from 25 Powerful Pondering Questions
- Seeing or Revealing Me Chart (Character: **Noah**)

> Limited time for reviewing home-work so time will be given to Miracles. Start working on these, if time permits. Complete the rest for homework.

- Bible presentations (selected students) _____
  Homework adjustment, if any: _____
  _____
  _____

Date : _____

SESSION 6

- Bible presentations
- Review homework from session 5
- Miracle - Two Demonic Cured

- 5th – 5 questions from 25 Powerful Pondering Questions
- Seeing or Revealing Me Chart (Character: **Abraham**)

> Limited time for reviewing home-work so time will be given to Miracles. Start working on these, if time permits. Complete the rest for homework.

- Bible presentations (selected students) _____
  Homework adjustment, if any: _____
  _____
  _____

Date : _____

SESSION 7

- Bible presentations
- Review homework from session 5
- Miracle - Naaman Cured of Leprosy

- On a separate sheet of paper have them list strengths and virtue from worksheets
- Seeing or Revealing Me Chart (Character: **Sarah**)
- Writing presentation ("About Me") Due in three weeks (Session 10)

> Limited time for reviewing home-work so time will be given to Miracles. Start working on these, if time permits. Complete the rest for homework.

- Bible presentations (selected students)_____
  Homework adjustment, if any:_____
  _____
  _____

Date : _____

SESSION 8

- Bible presentations
- Miracle – Increase of the Widow's Oil

- A study of II Peter 1:3-11 (Start on this. Have them complete it for homework)
- Work on "About Me" presentation in class (as time permits)

> Limited time for reviewing home-work so time will be given to Miracles. Start working on these, if time permits. Complete the rest for homework.

- Bible presentations (selected students)_____
  Homework adjustment, if any:_____
  _____
  _____

13

Date : _____

SESSION 9

- Bible presentations
- Finish up II Peter 1:3-11 and discuss
- Miracle - Miracle- Elisha Prophesies Plenty in Samaria   {If time doesn't permit you to complete this, then finish it in Session 10}
- Work on "About Me" presentation in class (as time permits) It's due next session!
- Bible presentations (selected students)_____
  Homework adjustment, if any: _____
  _____

Date : _____

SESSION 10

- Bible presentations
- "About Me" presentation
- Survey & Personal Evaluation Questions
- Bible presentations (selected students)_____
  Homework adjustment, if any:_____
  _____
  _____

Date : _____

SESSION 11

- _____
- _____
- _____
- _____
- Bible presentations (selected students)_____
  Homework adjustment, if any:_____
  _____
  _____

Date : _____

SESSION 12 (Exit – no homework)

- _____
- _____
- _____
   _____
   _____

Date:_____
Session:_____

Miracle – Water made wine in Cana
John 2: 1 – 11

Was it an occurrence of nature?

_____

Jesus did not touch the water nor gave it a verbal command.
How do you suppose it happen?

_____
_____

What does this miracle tell us about Jesus? The kingdom? The supernatural?

_____
_____
_____

I believe there were something more going on in the spirit realm of communication between Mary and Jesus that caused her to say **v. 5** and Jesus instructing **v7**. Her faith caused Him to move from the man (flesh) Jesus, into the God (Spirit) Jesus. She knew the power that was within Him. I believe He pick up on something from her that say it's time to start manifesting the glory – so He yield!

The Mind

("For as the heavens are higher than the earth, so are my ways higher than your ways, and my thoughts than your thoughts" Isaiah 55: 9)

From this verse we understand that God operates in the thought realm. Is it possible that Jesus just imagined seeing wine in the pots rather than water? That through belief, an image, and feelings a miracle manifested. Since He is sovereign, He controlled the acceleration of the manifestation.

The Subconscious (spirit mind) is home for :
- Belief
- Thoughts
- Feelings

Let's apply these 3 to the Water made wine.

<u>Belief:</u>
We know that Jesus believed that this could happen, because He is the One who said, "If thou canst believe, all things are possible to him that believe [Mark9:23; *and other verses*] We know He believed in miracles because He was a Miracle.

Thought/Image
Isaiah 55: 9 shows us that He thinks. & **Psalm 139:17** "How precious also are thy thoughts unto me. O God! How great is the sum of them!"
He created us in His image. He gave us a mind to do what His does. His is just more perfect! 😊
"…… But we have the mind of Christ" **I Corinth. 2:16**

Feelings/Mood
The marriage celebration creates the right mood. Emotions runs high. High joy – pure joy – sweet joy -ecstasy. The mood at a marriage is usually contagious. [The fruit of *joy* – Gal.5:22]

contagious – 1. (of a disease)….
2. (of an emotion, feeling, or attitude) likely to spread to and affect others.

A union
When all three works in sync (belief, thought, feeling) in the process of creating, they become one - as consummating a marriage union where the two become one and brings forth a miracle.

Meditation exercise

Your imagination is a function of the eyes of your spirit mind. With your imagination you are going to see somewhat of the miracle of the wine making.

Close your eyes and imagine that you are at the wedding. You heard the laughter and feel the joy. You are now standing next to 6 water pots full of water. Now see the water slowly changing to a cherry color. As the water is changing, say in your own voice with a low slow rhythm "Miracles" 3 times as you see the color process completed. Now look across from where you are standing and see Jesus smiling at you and say Praise the Lord! You can now open your natural eyes.

Sounds and feelings add pulses. They wake up the powers within!
Our repeated rhythmic/rhythmatic thoughts act as a cooing for the 3 to become one. They (belief, rhythmatic thoughts,feelings) initiate a union. Each sends out living pulses or vibrations. The pulses or vibrations act as strong sexual chemicals. It is at this point that they become irresistible - and we know the rest of the story! 😊

The Urban Dictionary
cooing – For a guy to flirt, date, or attempt any verbal or physical relationship with a girl. Derived from the symbolism of animals using mating calls.

mating – the action of male and female animals having sex (or breeding) to reproduce, and procreate.

∧∧∧

Student: Pray a prayer related to this miracle.

Date:_____
Session:_____

Miracle – Creation of the World
Genesis 1: 1 - 27

> "Imitate God, therefore, in everything you do, because you are His dear children." Eph. 5:1

Before creating a miracle, it may start out with nothing more than a dream, desire, want, an idea, or just one big thought (a big picture). God wanted to create a world, but it wasn't created all at one time. He went through phases or steps of creating it. He knew He would need something solid and concrete that would support his world for as long as He desire it to remain. He built it on a solid foundation. A workable foundation. This one big giant living planet/organism. He saw or imagine everything His world would need and He put everything in place for the maintenance of it. He started with heaven -- which could refer to atmosphere or the universe with all its planets -- and a secure foundation [Earth], much like a builder does with a house or building.

****

The Earth was without form
[vv.2,3]

The outer view or physical view of your desired miracle starts out "without physical form" and may appears to be unusable or hard to construct in tangible form. You only have an image in your mind. You see it in the mind as easy to do, but the unfolding of it in the natural present some obstacles or something negative rises up. It may seem without form, void, and unusable in this present time. But still, you envision how to get from point A to point B! As you move from point A to point B you have to imagine and confess that, that obstacle/problem is dissolved.

It was dark all over! But then there were a movement of the Spirit, and God spoke; He gave a command and <u>light appeared</u>. In order for us to see our miracle stages progressing physically we need to see some evident of it evolving. We need light! The Lord will shine light- *"Thou shalt also decree (order, command, decide, pronounce, prescribe) a thing, and it shall be established unto thee: <u>and the light shall shine upon thy ways</u>."* Job 22:28 KJB [*You will decide on a matter, and it will be established for you, and light will shine on your ways!* Job 22:28 NLT] [*"For You will light my lamp; The LORD my God will enlighten my darkness."* Ps. 18:28 NKJV] Our light comes from spoken words! I need to keep seeing it in the light of the Word in faith and in my spirit mind [calling/speaking those things which are not as though they were/exist already – Romans 4:17,{ "I AM …"}]. Words are spirits of life or death. Curses or blessings. God spoke words to His vision. We have to speak to ours; the written Word, declarations, affirmations, etc. When we keep working the Word, the Light will shine and guide us in the ways we should go that we may see progressive evident or view it manifesting.

To form our miracle, we have to do some seeing and speaking. God visualized (saw) what He wanted, then spoke it into existence.

He needed some light, not that He couldn't see what He was doing, but that we could see what He did [God is light] and follow His example [Imitate Him].

He kept seeing the vision as it was forming into shape. Keep meditation on the vision. Keep it before your eyes. Keep speaking in faith. Be persistent, consistent, and patient. There will come an unfolding of it in God's predetermined time.

Meditation Exercise

This may seem like a long exercise, but it is not long compared to God creating it in 6 days. This exercise will help awaken or stirs your imagination, strengthen it, and possibly come to better recognize God's voice.

Close your eyes and imagine that you are seeing God create the world.

First, See a dark Earth, and an atmosphere with other planets.
See the Spirit of God moving as a cloud as bright as the sun.

Day 1

Now hear God say, "Let there be Day.
Now see Night without moon and stars.
Now see Day again without a sun.

Day 2

Now hear God say "Let there be a sky. See sky with clouds.

Day 3

Hear God say, "Let dry land, seas, plants and trees appear -see them.

Day 4

Hear God say, "Let the sun, moon and starts appear in the sky of heaven – see them in the second heaven (way up above the clouds).

Day 5

Hear God say, "Let creatures that live in the sea appear – see them (fishes, seals, whales, octopus); and creatures that fly in the sky; see them (birds, eagles, ravens, doves).

Day 6

Hear God say, "Let cattle, creeping things, and beast appear – see them (sheep, cows, horses, bugs, ants, grasshoppers, elephants, hippos, apes) [God saw that it was all good] Hear Him say -- All Good!

Now hear God say, "Let us make a man in our image, after our likeness. See Adam being formed from the ground with life in Him. Now see him falling asleep and God miraculous removing a rib from him without surgery. Now see Eve lying next to Adam. Now see them both standing looking with awe of each other.

The work of creation is completed. Now hear God say "It is very good!". Try seeing as much of creation as you can before opening your eyes; and say "Praise God for Creation!"

^^^^^^^^^^^^^^^^^^^

Student: Pray a prayer related to this miracle.

Date:_____
Session:_____

Miracle – 10 Plagues in Egypt
Referred to by God as multiplied wonders -- 11:9,10
Exodus, Chapters 7 - 10

> "**Imitate God,** therefore, in everything you do, because you are His dear children."   Eph. 5:1

Aaron's rod used to:

1st – Turn water to blood [7:17]
2nd – Cause the waters to bring forth frogs [8:5]
3rd – Turn dust to lice [8:17]

God's Hand:

4th – God sends swarms of flies – [8:21-24]
5th – God strikes Egypt's beast with a killer disease [9:3-7]
6th – God turn ashes into a boil plague [9:8-12]

Moses' rod used to:

7th – Release hail in Egypt [9:23]
8th – Release an East wind that released locust [10:13]

Was rod used? It does not mention one!

9th – Moses stretch hand toward heaven. Thick darkness appeared 3 days in all Egypt. [10:22,23]

God's Hand

10th – God sends death plague throughout Egypt. [12:29]

Some of these wonders God allowed Moses and Aaron to join in: some He didn't. It still required them to have Faith in God or the God kind of Faith.

If God used different things that came from Earth's substance to open up portals to the supernatural realm, then we shouldn't find it strange, impossible, or find fault that He would use the **mind** to do the same [to open a portal to release the supernatural into the Earth realm]. The **mind (portal)** of man is in an earthen vessel. We have read in the Bible that He has uses other things, such as: oil, prayer shawl, handkerchiefs, and even a shadow, etc. He can use whatever method or thing He choose; we just have to join and obey Him in faith when He tells us to do this or do that. Use this or use that.

> *portal* – 1. a doorway, gate, or other entrance, especially a large and imposing one. 3. The approach or entrance to a bridge or tunnel.
>
> *Similar*: doorway, door, gateway, gate, entrance, opening.

To Whom or what do you suppose our minds are link?

_____

Wisdom from the Spirit of God

⁶ "Howbeit we speak wisdom among the perfect: yet a wisdom not of this world, nor of the rulers of this world, which are coming to nought: ⁷but we speak God's wisdom in a mystery, even the wisdom that hath been hidden, which God foreordained before the worlds unto our glory: ⁸which none of the rulers of this world knoweth: for had they known it, they would not have crucified the Lord of glory:

⁹but as it is written, Things which eye saw not, and ear heard not, And which entered not into the heart of man, Whatsoever things God prepared for them that love him.

¹⁰But unto us God revealed them through the Spirit: for the Spirit searcheth all things, yea, the deep things of God. ¹¹For who among men knoweth the things of a man, save the spirit of the man, which is in him? even so the things of God none knoweth, save the Spirit of God. ¹²But we received, not the spirit of the world, but the spirit which is of God; that we might know the things that are freely given to us by God. ¹³Which things also we speak, not in words which man's wisdom teacheth, but which the Spirit teacheth; comparing spiritual things with spiritual.

¹⁴Now the natural man receiveth not the things of the Spirit of God: for they are foolishness unto him; and he cannot know them, because they are spiritually judged. ¹⁵But he that is spiritual judgeth all things, and he himself is judged of no man. ¹⁶For who hath known the mind of the Lord, that he should instruct him? **But we have the mind of Christ**." I Corinth. 2:6-16

****

Meditation Exercise:

List 5 of your desires:
_____
_____
_____
_____
_____

Close your eyes, take a deep breath and slowly release it. Now imagine that you are standing on Earth near a river (put yourself in the picture filled with joy/gladness). Now look toward the sky. As you look, you see a portal opening in the heavenly. Now see from your list one of your desires followed by another in order - You are happy! As each one comes through, say "Miracles" in your own voice with a low slow rhythm "Miracles". For instant you may see your desired position in life, see it transferring in joy as you say, "Miracles" see your next desire being transferred in joy as you say "Miracles", etc. At the end, before opening your eyes, say "Hallelujah" Thank You Lord! I received it!

∧∧∧∧∧∧∧∧∧∧∧∧∧∧∧∧∧∧∧∧

Student: Pray a prayer related to this miracle.

Date:_____
Session:_____

Miracle – Draught of Fishes
Luke 5:1 - 11

> **"Imitate God,** therefore, in everything you do, because you are His dear children." Eph. 5:1

In this miracle we see that Simon and his partners had worked all night and caught nothing. Surely, they had to be feeling some sort of way knowing this could put their livelihood at risk. The thought must have played out in their minds, "What if we don't catch any tomorrow night, or the next night? What if we don't ever catch any again?" The big, WHAT IF?"
Can you name 1 or 2 of your big, WHAT Ifs" (negative or positive) and the result or outcome. If the outcome/result is negative, what is your back-up plan?

1) What if _____

    Result/Outcome_____

    Back-up plan_____

2) What if _____

    Result/Outcome_____

    Back-up plan_____

****

Simon didn't know that Jesus had a plan in mind when He got in his boat. What was Jesus' first instruction to Simon?

1)_____

What was Jesus' second instruction to Simon?

2)_____

Simon answered, "Master, we have toiled all night and took nothing! [Simon's belief was that the "best catch" was at nighttime (his faith was in a system: night fishing). But when the best system or method, etc. doesn't work; then you need a miracle!

⁵And Simon answered, "Master, we toiled all night and took nothing! But at your word I will let down the nets."

What impression of Simon do you get from his response to Jesus?

3)_____

_____

22

4) How did Simon get his surprised miracle? _____

It took one man's obedience to set a miracle in motion.

Simon saw that the best catch didn't come because of his belief system, but because of his obedience.

Our belief has to be opened up to God's obedience.

Simon's thinking was probably "This not going to work, but I'll do it. We need some fishes"!

This action was designed to change Simon and the others way of thinking and believing.

When Jesus gets on the boat with us, we have to be willing to change our way of thinking and belief.

This was their first personal encounter with faith or putting faith in God and not just in a belief system.

Jesus has to be the foundation of our beliefs.

THE BEST CATCH

Simon's "best catch" was when Jesus got in the boat. That encounter initiated a change in his life and his way of thinking!

5) What does Simon's <u>nets</u> represent in your life?

Spiritual_____

Personal_____

What does the <u>water</u> represent in your life?

Spiritual_____

Personal_____

Example: For a business person <u>the nets</u> could represent the **tools** he uses to catch clients: business cards, advertising, flyer, the media, etc.

The <u>water</u> could represent a target community or group.

Example: For a Christian, nets could represent faith, time, sacrifice, discipline, mind, etc.

Example: Personal nets could represent mindset, disposition, type of spirit, such as, laziness, stubborn; nature, etc.

Water represents – the word, the Holy Spirit, life, the world, etc. [Water has many symbolized meanings.]

Nets are used to catch something (good or bad). It may have other meanings, but in this lesson, we referring to Simon's nets.

6) What net/s do you need to toss out into what water to get a catch? Or stop tossing out to prevent a catch?

A better way to understand this is "You reap what you sow"!

_____

_____

∧∧∧∧∧∧∧∧∧∧∧∧∧∧∧∧∧∧∧∧∧∧∧∧∧∧∧∧

In the disciple second catch, I want to point out that they catch **153 large fish**. I believe the Lord want us to expect large miracles and great catches. Have great expectation of great things! Don't set low goals! Set goals in faith!

7) Short knowledge: Biblical numbers meaning –

#1 _____

#5 _____

#3 _____

#9 [1+5+3] _____

****

Meditation Exercise: Simon's boat has become your boat

Close your eyes, take a deep breath and slowly release it. Now imagine the scene. You are in a large boat close to the lake shore. You see a crowd of people gathered to hear Jesus. Now see Jesus walking away from the crowd toward your boat. He gets in, sat down, and tells you to move out a little from the land. See Him facing the crowd and saying, "Blessed are the poor in spirit, for theirs is the kingdom of heaven!" He raises His right hand and dismisses the crowd, saying, "May the LORD bless and keep you!" He now turns to you and say, "Move out into the deep and let down your net for a catch" You steer your boat out far from land. You say to the Lord, "Lord, I been toiling for a long time in prayer and waiting in faith for change, but haven't see any! But at your word I will let down the net. You now toss the net overboard and wait. And when it seems like nothing was going to happen, you suddenly see a lot of activity going on with your net. You start to pull the net up with great anticipation (joy) as supernatural strength enters into you. As you pull your net abroad, you see all your desires in it. After it is on board, you turn to Jesus and fall on your knees in worship, saying, "Truly you are King of kings, and Lord of Lord, Alpha and Omega, the Great I AM"! Take a few more moments in worship before opening your eyes.

∧∧∧∧∧∧∧∧∧∧∧∧∧∧∧∧∧∧

Student: Pray a prayer related to this miracle.

English Standard Version

Luke 5:1 – 11 [1ˢᵗ Catch]

¹On one occasion, while the crowd was pressing in on him to hear the word of God, he was standing by the lake of Gennesaret, ²and he saw two boats by the lake, but the fishermen had gone out of them and were washing their nets. ³Getting into one of the boats, which was Simon's, he asked him to put out a little from the land. And he sat down and taught the people from the boat. ⁴And when he had finished speaking, he said to Simon, "Put out into the deep and let down your nets for a catch." ⁵And Simon answered, "Master, we toiled all night and took nothing! But at your word I will let down the nets." ⁶And when they had done this, they enclosed a large number of fish, and their nets were breaking. ⁷They signaled to their partners in the other boat to come and help them. And they came and filled both the boats, so that they began to sink. ⁸But when Simon Peter saw it, he fell down at Jesus' knees, saying, "Depart from me, for I am a sinful man, O Lord." ⁹For he and all who were with him were astonished at the catch of fish that they had taken, ¹⁰and so also were James and John, sons of Zebedee, who were partners with Simon. And Jesus said to Simon, "Do not be afraid; from now on you will be catching men."[a] ¹¹And when they had brought their boats to land, they left everything and followed him.

John 21: 1- 14 [2ⁿᵈ Catch]

¹After this Jesus revealed himself again to the disciples by the Sea of Tiberias, and he revealed himself in this way. ²Simon Peter, Thomas (called the Twin), Nathanael of Cana in Galilee, the sons of Zebedee, and two others of his disciples were together. ³Simon Peter said to them, "I am going fishing." They said to him, "We will go with you." They went out and got into the boat, but that night they caught nothing.

⁴Just as day was breaking, Jesus stood on the shore; yet the disciples did not know that it was Jesus. ⁵Jesus said to them, "Children, do you have any fish?" They answered him, "No." ⁶He said to them, "Cast the net on the right side of the boat, and you will find some." So they cast it, and now they were not able to haul it in, because of the quantity of fish. ⁷That disciple whom Jesus loved therefore said to Peter, "It is the Lord!" When Simon Peter heard that it was the Lord, he put on his outer garment, for he was stripped for work, and threw himself into the sea. ⁸The other disciples came in the boat, dragging the net full of fish, for they were not far from the land, but about a hundred yards[a] off.

⁹When they got out on land, they saw a charcoal fire in place, with fish laid out on it, and bread. ¹⁰Jesus said to them, "Bring some of the fish that you have just caught." ¹¹So Simon Peter went aboard and hauled the net ashore, **full of large fish, 153 of them.** And although there were so many, the net was not torn. ¹²Jesus said to them, "Come and have breakfast." Now none of the disciples dared ask him, "Who are you?" They knew it was the Lord. ¹³Jesus came and took the bread and gave it to them, and so with the fish. ¹⁴This was now the third time that Jesus was revealed to the disciples after he was raised from the dead.

Date:_____
Session:_____

Miracle – Two Demoniac Cured:
Battles In the Mind
Mark 5:1 – 20; Matt. 8:28 - 34; Luke 8:26 - 39

> **"Imitate God,** therefore, in everything you do, because you are His dear children." Eph. 5:1
>
> "And these signs will accompany those who believe: in my name they will cast out demons;…" Mark 16:17

Insight

There were 2 men possessed with a great company of demons, named Legion, but because the head demon spoke from one of the men, they considered him captain. So, in Mark and Luke's account their focus was on the man whom the captain spoke through. They both could have had equal number of demons or the demons just keep moving from one man to the other man. These demons were torturing each other mentally fighting over who was going to stay in these bodies and who was going to leave. These poor men were experiencing the effects of the demons' battles within their minds. They kept them as close to Death as they could – the graveyard. These demons (Legion) fights for territory but none of them ever wins, because their war is always among themselves – it's not in them to win. They don't even have it in them to volunteer or voluntarily leave. They refuse to relinquish their rights, because it's not in them to do so.

But when Jesus came, **all** of them had to go - involuntarily! They didn't want to go out of the country probably because there were demons eviler and more destructive than them that they would have to encounter.

1) What do you think or your insight why they didn't want to leave that country?
_____
_____

The murdering thought of these demons caused these men to commit acts of suicide. They didn't care if the men killed themselves or not, they were not going to surrender to each other. It was by the grace and mercy of God; the men's acts of suicide were not successful. We know that a compassionate Jesus saw them, before coming to them to show forth His glory.

> Wild thought!
>
> Because the devil has the power of death, could it be that Legion didn't want the men to die so that they could remain in their bodies. They did say they didn't want to leave out the country. But all the same, the credit and glory goes to God, because He has power and control over demons.

We know somewhat of what was going on in these men's mind and who was influencing them to act out. Legion affected the men's thoughts which reflected in the men's actions. Their minds were darkened by reason of the demons. They were men without hope in the world! They had severe cases of "bottom thoughts".

Some of their possible "bottom thoughts":
a) no hope of any kind
b) never ever being freed
c) never ever conquering.
d) never ever rising to the tops

2) Can you recall a "bottom thought" you have experience - past or present- or one that you are working on now?

Do /Did they plague you?

_____

Do you still experience them? If so, how do you handle or manage them?

_____

3) Do you see your mind ever being free from them? If you answered yes, then that is good as long as you are taking <u>action.</u>

If you don't see yourself as ever being free, then you have surrendered your power to not being free.

People in bonds are not liberated to move forward or further.

Today we will see ourselves free!

****

Meditation Exercise:

Close your eyes, take a deep breath and slowly release it. Now imagine this scene. You are dressed in Biblical clothing sitting at the tomb of Jesus, crying, and looking in an empty tomb. You perceive that someone has appeared. You turn and see Jesus. You rise, run to Him, fall at His feet crying: LORD! Jesus places His right hand on your head and says "Woman be healed of thine plagues". You sense a calm of peace and freedom. Your face lights up as He takes your hand helping you rise. You know you have been delivered. You praise and thank Him. He tells you to "Go home to your family and friends and tell them how much the Lord has done for you, and how he has had mercy on you." He vanishes from your present. You leave the area of the tomb running and rejoicing! You can now open your eyes!

∧∧∧∧∧∧∧∧∧∧∧∧∧∧∧∧∧∧∧∧

Student: Pray a prayer related to this miracle.

Mark 5: 1 – 20 [Jesus Heals a Man with a Demon]

[1]They came to the other side of the sea, to the country of the Gerasenes. [2]And when Jesus had stepped out of the boat, immediately there met him out of the tombs a man with an unclean spirit. [3]He lived among the tombs. And no one could bind him anymore, not even with a chain, [4]for he had often been bound with shackles and chains, but he wrenched the chains apart, and he broke the shackles in pieces. No one had the strength to subdue him. [5]Night and day among the tombs and on the mountains he was always crying out and cutting himself with stones. [6]And when he saw Jesus from afar, he ran and fell down before him. [7]And crying out with a loud voice, he said, "What have you to do with me, Jesus, Son of the Most High God? I adjure you by God, do not torment me." [8]For he was saying to him, "Come out of the man, you unclean spirit!" [9]And Jesus asked him, "What is your name?" He replied, "My name is Legion, for we are many." [10]And he begged him earnestly not to send them out of the country. [11]Now a great herd of pigs was feeding there on the hillside, [12]and they begged him, saying, "Send us to the pigs; let us enter them." [13]So he gave them permission. And the unclean spirits came out and entered the pigs; and the herd, numbering about two thousand, rushed down the steep bank into the sea and drowned in the sea.

[14]The herdsmen fled and told it in the city and in the country. And people came to see what it was that had happened. [15]And they came to Jesus and saw the demon-possessed man, the one who had had the legion, sitting there, clothed and in his right mind, and they were afraid. [16]And those who had seen it described to them what had happened to the demon-possessed man and to the pigs. [17]And they began to beg Jesus to depart from their region. [18]As he was getting into the boat, the man who had been possessed with demons begged him that he might be with him. [19]And he did not permit him but said to him, "Go home to your friends and tell them how much the Lord has done for you, and how he has had mercy on you." [20]And he went away and began to proclaim in the Decapolis how much Jesus had done for him, and everyone marveled.

Jesus Heals Two Men with Demons [Matt. 8:28-34]

[28]And when he came to the other side, to the country of the Gadarenes, two demon-possessed men met him, coming out of the tombs, so fierce that no one could pass that way. [29]And behold, they cried out, "What have you to do with us, O Son of God? Have you come here to torment us before the time?" [30]Now a herd of many pigs was feeding at some distance from them. [31]And the demons begged him, saying, "If you cast us out, send us away into the herd of pigs." [32]And he said to them, "Go." So they came out and went into the pigs, and behold, the whole herd rushed down the steep bank into the sea and drowned in the waters. [33]The herdsmen fled, and going into the city they told everything, especially what had happened to the demon-possessed men. [34]And behold, all the city came out to meet Jesus, and when they saw him, they begged him to leave their region.

Date:_____
Session:_____

Miracle – Naaman Cured of Leprosy
II Kings 5:1 - 16

> **"Imitate God,** therefore, in everything you do, because you are His dear children." Eph. 5:1
>
> "…even God, who quickeneth the dead, and calleth those things which be not as though they were." Romans 4:17

" ¹ Now Naaman, captain of the host of the king of Syria, was a great man with his master, and honourable, because by him the LORD had given deliverance unto Syria: he was also a mighty man in valour, but he was a leper. ²And the Syrians had gone out by companies, and had brought away captive out of the land of Israel a little maid; and she waited on Naaman's wife. ³And she said unto her mistress, Would God my lord were with the prophet that is in Samaria! for he would recover him of his leprosy. ⁴And one went in, and told his lord, saying, Thus and thus said the maid that is of the land of Israel. ⁵And the king of Syria said, Go to, go, and I will send a letter unto the king of Israel. And he departed, and took with him ten talents of silver, and six thousand pieces of gold, and ten changes of raiment.

⁶And he brought the letter to the king of Israel, saying, Now when this letter is come unto thee, behold, I have therewith sent Naaman my servant to thee, that thou mayest recover him of his leprosy. ⁷And it came to pass, when the king of Israel had read the letter, that he rent his clothes, and said, Am I God, to kill and to make alive, that this man doth send unto me to recover a man of his leprosy? wherefore consider, I pray you, and see how he seeketh a quarrel against me.

⁸And it was so, when Elisha the man of God had heard that the king of Israel had rent his clothes, that he sent to the king, saying, Wherefore hast thou rent thy clothes? let him come now to me, and he shall know that there is a prophet in Israel. ⁹So Naaman came with his horses and with his chariot, and stood at the door of the house of Elisha. ¹⁰And Elisha sent a messenger unto him, saying, Go and wash in Jordan seven times, and thy flesh shall come again to thee, and thou shalt be clean. ¹¹But Naaman was wroth, and went away, and said, Behold, I thought, He will surely come out to me, and stand, and call on the name of the LORD his God, and strike his hand over the place, and recover the leper. ¹²Are not Abana and Pharpar, rivers of Damascus, better than all the waters of Israel? may I not wash in them, and be clean? So he turned and went away in a rage. ¹³And his servants came near, and spake unto him, and said, My father, if the prophet had bid thee do some great thing, wouldest thou not have done it? how much rather then, when he saith to thee, Wash, and be clean? ¹⁴Then went he down, and dipped himself seven times in Jordan, according to the saying of the man of God: and his flesh came again like unto the flesh of a little child, and he was clean.

vv. 1,2
(Characters: Naaman, little maid, & you)

A) Naaman, was a captain of an army. He was great and honorable (special favor) with his king. He was a leper. By him the LORD gave Syria victory over Israel.

B) The little maid from Israel
- Servant to Naaman's wife
- Though she was a captive, she had compassion on Naaman and his wife.

This little maid had every right to be bitter and close her heart up from feeling compassion on Naaman and his wife. After all, they had taken her from her family, friends, country, her dream, and everything that she loved.

1. How do you see Jesus in her?

   _____
   _____
   _____

2. As young children, that is when we first profess what we want to be when we grow up. As little children we didn't know there were a process of becoming. At the age you are now what question/s would you have asked yourself back then, if you knew it was a process to find out if the dream was attainable/reachable of that little child of many ages ago? If you have many questions, please write them on a separate sheet of paper.

   _____
   _____
   _____
   _____

3. (a)Has your little child dream changed? (b)If so, what caused it to change and what has it changed to?

   _____
   _____
   _____
   _____

4. (a)Have the questions in #2 changed by the answer you supplied for question #3? (b)Can you still ask those same questions and answer them? If the questions have changed, write them down and answer them on a separate sheet of paper.

   _____
   _____
   _____

5. Where are you at now in that dream? Such as; living it, pursuing it, nowhere, it died, or that is not what God wanted me to do/be.

   _____
   _____
   _____

6. Do we suppose things changed for the little maid when Naaman return home: healed and converted?

   _____
   _____

There is a possibility that God had a divine plan for her like that of Joseph. That after she had passed the tests, He would take her beyond what she had dream. God's divine plan/ or dream is higher than our dreams.

v.3
(First connection)

The little maid was Naaman's connection to his healing. She had confidence/faith in the prophets' ability to perform miracles. She was a little maid with king size faith. God arranges connections to miracle and what He calls us to. If it takes a company of people, then God will arrange them to connect.

7. Do you sense that God is making connections in your life to bring you into your true destiny? If so, what do you perceive or see taking place?

___

vv. 6,7
(The interception)

The king of Syria sent the letter to the king of Israel and didn't make mention of Elisha the prophet. Naaman never met Elisha, so he didn't know what he looked like. Naaman trusted what the king had written concerning him being sent to the prophet. If the king had a seal on the letter, then Naaman couldn't open it; therefore, he didn't know exactly what was written.

Demonic forces work to intercept miracles and prayers. [Daniel 10th chapter].

intercept – to stop, seize, or interrupt in progress or course, or before arrival.

Naaman learned something about his king that day - that maybe his king honored him and showed him favor as long as he was winning battles, but personally he did not care for him at all. He had come a long way to get his healing and the king was about to make him miss it.

The king of Syria sent him to a king, but this king was inadequate for what Naaman needed. He was a man of statute, but he didn't have the kind of power that Naaman needed.

From this we see that he encountered a flesh source, before a spiritual source. The enemy tried to intercept it. God did not allow Naaman to miss his miracle. He provided another connection. Someone who had connection to the prophet Elisha.

8. When it's your turn to walk into your miracle or destiny do you have 'resting faith' in our Almighty God that He has arrange everything and will oversee it until you are living in it?

___

v.8
(Second connection)

Naaman's connection went to Elisha and told him about the letter and the king's reaction. Elisha said, "Bring him (Naaman) to me and he will know that there is a prophet in Israel. Elisha knew his calling and the power for miracle that flowed through him. They were so common to him that he could speak with such confidence, assurance, boldness, of the results.

v.9,10
(Naaman's first connection sent him to a place, but the second connection into Elisha's presence.)

When Naaman arrived at Elisha's house, he went to the door, but Elisha didn't come to greet him. He sent a messenger unto him saying, "Go and wash in Jordan seven times, and thy flesh shall come again to thee, and thou shalt be clean." Elisha remained out of Naaman's view, but he sent a word that he had confident and assurance in that it would work. This is an illustration of God sending his word to heal us and deliver us from destruction - [He sent his word to heal -Psalm 107:20] Jesus is the word. He gave him a word by way of an instruction.

9. [a]If God wants us to take part in the unfolding of dreams or the miracle process, will he guide us, instruct us, and lead us in the way we should go? [b]In what ways have you sense God directing you to do something? Such as a prompting in your spirit, showing you in a dream, through instructions, speaking through someone else, etc.?

_____
_____
_____
_____

v. 11,12
(God's timing)

Our miracles may not come how we expect them or in the timeframe we expect them. If we expect miracle to be done our way and our time, we could miss them. We have to wait on God and give Him space to work.

10. What happens when we tried to go ahead of God or move out of His will, or take matters into our own hands?

_____
_____
_____
_____

v. 13,14
(Miracle blockers)

Naaman didn't want to do what the prophet told him to do. He didn't want to humble himself. He felt like he may have been better than that (though he was a leper). Pride manifested. He saw the Jordan's water worse than his leprosy.

When he saw what he had to do to get his miracle, he said, "No" in rage. He was very frustrated! I suppose Naaman felt very let down by the king. A man he honored and probable though they were pretty tight. And then, to arrive at Elisha's house - right at his door - and Elisha would not even come to the door. He had come all that way just to be treated unfairly and then told to go dip in less than favorable water than back at home. (He was sooo in his flesh and emotions!)

His servants understood he was having a very bad day. They calm him down and caused him to come to his senses again, or miss his miracle. With having nothing to lose and to make the journey back home wondering if it would have work, he carried out the command. He saw that it was wise to do it God's way!

> 11. What are you willing to lay aside to get the assistance of Heaven so you can walk in your dream or the destiny God has for you?
>
> _____
> _____
> _____
> _____

v. 15 – 18
(A change)

After that miracle, Naaman was converted and acknowledged that there were only one God in all the Earth and that God was in Israel.

_____

Meditation Exercise:

Imagine you are dressed in Biblical days and you are sitting on a beautiful white horse at Elisha's house. You descend off the horse. Walking to his house, you are now standing at his door. You have come a long way to be free from what plague you, for you have been sent there. You are excited because this is your day, not only to be freed, but also see the famous prophet, Elisha. A message was sent before you, so Elisha already knows why you are here. His servant greets you at the door and says, "Elisha says to go dip 7 times in Jordan and you'll be delivered/healed." You're excited but also a little disappointed because you didn't get to see Elisha. You mount on your horse and head to the Jordan River. You arrive there and looks at the river. Your thought: "The water does not look favorable, but I have come a long way and I have dealt with this thing for a long time; therefore, the Jordan does not look so bad. You see it now as your hope!" You descend off your horse and head into the water until it reaches chest height. You start dipping and counting: 1, 2 , 3, 4, 5, 6, 7! Standing and walking out the water you sense a heavy weigh has been lifted. You look toward Heaven and see the Holy Spirit in the form of a dove of radiant glory descend. He encircles you flying from head to toe. The glory from His presence fills your soul with brightness and so much love, peace, and joy [see the inside of you filled with sunlight]! Just bask in His presence a little worshiping and thanking Him. [**Pause**]. You see the glory dove ascends back into the heavenly and you are left rejoicing and worshipping. You are now free. Mount back on your horse, and ride in the wind enjoying your freedom. You see a blue cloud in front of you. Ride into it. Now open your eyes.

^^^^^^^^^^^^^^^^^^^^^^^^^^^^^^^^^^^^^^^

Student pray a prayer related to miracle.

Date:_____
Session:_____

Miracle – Increase of the Widow's Oil
II Kings 4:1 - 7

> **"Imitate God,** therefore, in everything you do, because you are His dear children."   Eph. 5:1

¹Now the wife of one of the sons of the prophets cried to Elisha, "Your servant my husband is dead, and you know that your servant feared the Lord, but the creditor has come to take my two children to be his slaves." ²And Elisha said to her, "What shall I do for you? Tell me; what have you in the house?" And she said, "Your servant has nothing in the house except a jar of oil." ³Then he said, "Go outside, borrow vessels from all your neighbors, empty vessels and not too few. ⁴Then go in and shut the door behind yourself and your sons and pour into all these vessels. And when one is full, set it aside." ⁵So she went from him and shut the door behind herself and her sons. And as she poured, they brought the vessels to her. ⁶When the vessels were full, she said to her son, "Bring me another vessel." And he said to her, "There is not another." Then the oil stopped flowing. ⁷She came and told the man of God, and he said, "Go, sell the oil and pay your debts, and you and your sons can live on the rest." II Kings 4:1-7 ESV

Miracle

In this miracle we see that this widow's husband was a prophet and servant to Elisha. Her husband was their source of income. Any money that he left them had run out and they were in a dire situation. She did the only thing she knew to do - Go to the man of God that her husband served! Her husband probably said to her, "After I'm gone, and if you ever need a miracle go to the man of God whom I have sown into, He will know what to do." (Note: It is a possibility that she sown into Elisha's ministry as well, such as baking bread or cooking a full meal for her husband to carry to Elisha. Chances are she tried to carry on her service to him for the sake of her husband's honor for as long as she could, until the meal, flour, and other items were depleted.)

This prophet gave into the prophetic and now his widow wife needed a miracle. She came to reap from where they/her husband had sown. God gave her an overflow of what here late husband had stored up in the kingdom from his/their service to Elisha. God greatly reward this widow for their faithful service.

We know that God still moves through prophets, but our first cry is to Him.

From verse 3 & 4 we can conclude that this was a special miracle just for that household. Elisha didn't tell her to invite or bring her neighbors or tell them what she was up to. They were instructed to ask only for empty vessels and go inside and close the door.

1) If neighbors would have looked inside and saw what was going on, what kind of reaction you think they would have had?

_____

2) What's your thoughts on why he told them to go inside and close the door?

_____

3) What can we expect from our faithfulness to the Lord?

_____

4) Besides faith, what does God generally gives us to release a miracle or partake of the supernatural?

_____

_____

5) Can God make these kinds of miracles available to everyone or to certain ones?

_____

Meditation Exercise:

Sit up straight, close your eyes, take a deep breath, and release it slowly. Now see you and your family sitting in a house. You hear a loud knock on your door. From the inside you ask who it is. They respond with a demand for $100,000 that you owe them, but don't have. They threaten to burn down your house and harm your children, if you don't have the money on a specific date. You cry out for mercy from God. He sends the prophet Elisha in your room. You tell Elisha about the threat. He asks you, "Do you have any money at all? You leave out the room and enter into one of the kids' room and grab some of their play money. You bring it to him and say, "God is my witness, this is the only thing we have that resembles money." He says to you "Place one of the paper bills in your Bible and after I'm gone, hold your Bible up to heaven and say, "My God shall supply all my needs according to His riches in glory." Then open your Bible. He vanishes and you carry out his instructions. You place the bill in your Bible, holds it up to heaven and confess, "My God shall supply all my needs according to His riches in glory." You then open your Bible and there is a check for a million dollars payable to you. Rejoice in praise for a moment before opening your eyes.

∧∧∧∧∧∧∧∧∧∧∧∧∧∧∧∧∧

Student: Pray a prayer related to this miracle.

Date:_____
Session:_____

Miracle – Elisha Prophesies Plenty in Samaria: Decision of the 4 Leprous
II Kings 7:1 – 9, 18-20

> **"Imitate God,** therefore, in everything you do, because you are His dear children." Eph. 5:1
>
> "…even God, who quickeneth the dead, and calleth those things which be not as though they were."
> Romans 4:17

¹Then Elisha said, Hear ye the word of the LORD; Thus saith the LORD, To morrow about this time *shall* a measure of fine flour *be sold* for a shekel, and two measures of barley for a shekel, in the gate of Samaria. ²Then a lord on whose hand the king leaned answered the man of God, and said, Behold, *if* the LORD would make windows in heaven, might this thing be? And he said, Behold, thou shalt see *it* with thine eyes, but shalt not eat thereof.

³And there were four leprous men at the entering in of the gate: and they said one to another, Why sit we here until we die? ⁴If we say, We will enter into the city, then the famine *is* in the city, and we shall die there: and if we sit still here, we die also. Now therefore come, and let us fall unto the host of the Syrians: if they save us alive, we shall live; and if they kill us, we shall but die. ⁵And they rose up in the twilight, to go unto the camp of the Syrians: and when they were come to the uttermost part of the camp of Syria, behold, *there was* no man there. ⁶For the Lord had made the host of the Syrians to hear a noise of chariots, and a noise of horses, *even* the noise of a great host: and they said one to another, Lo, the king of Israel hath hired against us the kings of the Hittites, and the kings of the Egyptians, to come upon us. ⁷Wherefore they arose and fled in the twilight, and left their tents, and their horses, and their asses, even the camp as it *was*, and fled for their life. ⁸And when these lepers came to the uttermost part of the camp, they went into one tent, and did eat and drink, and carried thence silver, and gold, and raiment, and went and hid *it*; and came again, and entered into another tent, and carried thence *also*, and went and hid *it*.

⁹Then they said one to another, We do not well: this day *is* a day of good tidings, and we hold our peace: if we tarry till the morning light, some mischief will come upon us: now therefore come, that we may go and tell the king's household.

¹⁰So they came and called unto the porter of the city: and they told them, saying, We came to the camp of the Syrians, and, behold, there was no man there, neither voice of man, but horses tied, and asses tied, and the tents as they were. ¹¹And he called the porters; and they told it to the king's house within. ¹²And the king arose in the night, and said unto his servants, I will now shew you what the Syrians have done to us. They know that we be hungry; therefore are they gone out of the camp to hide themselves in the field, saying, When they come out of the city, we shall catch them alive, and get into the city. ¹³And one of his servants answered and said, Let some take, I pray thee, five of the horses that remain, which are left in the city, (behold, they are as all the multitude of Israel that are left in it: behold, I say, they are even as all the multitude of the Israelites that are consumed:) and let us send and see. ¹⁴They took therefore two chariot horses; and the king sent after the host of the Syrians, saying, Go and see. ¹⁵And they went after them unto Jordan: and, lo, all the way was full of garments and vessels, which the Syrians had cast away in their haste. And the messengers returned,

and told the king. ¹⁶And the people went out, and spoiled the tents of the Syrians. So a measure of fine flour was sold for a shekel, and two measures of barley for a shekel, according to the word of the LORD. ¹⁷And the king appointed the lord on whose hand he leaned to have the charge of the gate: and the people trode upon him in the gate, and he died, as the man of God had said, who spake when the king came down to him.

¹⁸And it came to pass as the man of God had spoken to the king, saying, Two measures of barley for a shekel, and a measure of fine flour for a shekel, shall be tomorrow about this time in the gate of Samaria: ¹⁹And that lord answered the man of God, and said, Now, behold, *if* the LORD should make windows in heaven, might such a thing be? And he said, Behold, thou shalt see it with thine eyes, but shalt not eat thereof. ²⁰And so it fell out unto him: for the people trode upon him in the gate, and he died.

vv. 1, 2
The Prophecy

vv. 3,4,5
Four lepers situation

³And there were four leprous men at the entering in of the gate: and they said one to another, Why sit we here until we die? [Why are we waiting on Death]?

The lepers were sitting and waiting on Death, when God dropped a <u>notion</u> in them that it's not time to give up yet. Something rose up inside of them to make an effort to give it one more shot at staying alive. They were in a state of "The sentence of death is upon us. Let us die trying! They had to know if they did all they could to stay alive.

effort /n/ -- 2 : a serious attempt : Try

1) What benefit/s does effort produces?
_____
_____
_____
_____

When a teacher explains to a child how to work a problem to find the answer, but the child refuses to put forth the effort of attention and listening to understand they miss out on valuable information that could unlock another power that could propel them forward or have success in that subject. Potential could be there, but not effort.

The 4 lepers had a "label" upon them. They were unclean. They were feeling sorry for themselves. They didn't see the hidden potential among the 4 of them. They kept company with each other and that depressed, despondent, mediocre, spirit rested upon them all. God saw their current situation and say, "I want to use them". God will use the least likely person to set something awesome or amazing in motion.

depressed – in a state of general unhappiness or despondency.

despondent – in low spirits from loss of hope or courage.

Syn: disheartened, discouraged, dispirited, hopeless, downcast.

mediocre – of moderate or low quality, value, ability, or performance: not very good.

2) Have you or someone labeled you as un-useable? What label/s are you wearing, if any?
_____
_____

There is potential in you, and you may be aware of it, but there is something like a mark/s inside of you that tells you that you are not capable or insufficient to accomplish the task/assignment. It/They are like a hurdle/s, you just can't seem to jump over it/them. The lepers couldn't get pass their either, but that didn't stop God! The God of them rose up, and God will rise up in you above the hurdle to accomplish his purpose. For it will be accomplish by His sufficient, not your insufficient. "By the Spirit – Zech. 4:6

The lepers had to mentally rise up out of depression, despondence, and mediocre. They laid aside their uncleanness to find out what was out there - to know what did their future hold? I believe they placed their lives in God's hand, and started walking forward.

When they rose up mentally, they were able to rise up physically.

3) What is it that you have to mentally, emotionally, or/and physically rise up out of to travel into your future, or embrace your purpose/destiny?
_____
_____
_____
_____

The lepers knew that a hefty supply was in the Syrians' camp, but they didn't know if they would have to die early to find out. The lepers still carried the sentence of death upon them as they went forward. They were still in a state of dying by starvation. We like the lepers have to walk a daily life of death (die daily) to enter into what God has prepared. They were going to die of starvation before they died of leprosy, if they hadn't paid attention to that notion. We can suppose that some apprehension was present. We don't know if they went in faith, but we know that we have to move out in faith. We have to trust in God as He leads us into the unknown places.

4) Are there any apprehensions with you moving forward? If so, what is it/they?
_____
_____
_____
_____

Some folks have the fear of failing, some rejection, or some of losing control (a power loss). The fear of being uprooted from one state of being or state of existing to another state of being may be present. They fear transition. In the present state of being the essence of a person presence may seem to have control over some tangible and intangible power/spirts in their existence. There may be a fear there, that if they move, they lose. They may lose a secured spot. Too risky. When it comes to the fear of control, we have to turn the control over to God. And one day He may turn the reins over to us, under His watchful eye.

5) What frightens you about change? Change means we have to move out into the unknown, but we have to walk by faith and not by sight.
   _____
   _____
   _____
   _____

6) On a scale of 1 – 10, how fearful of you of change to better things for you or someone else?
   _____

7) (a) What is behind this apprehension listed in #4? (b) Why do you feel this apprehension? (c) Have you experience this apprehension before in wanting or desiring to rise and cause change?
   _____
   _____
   _____
   _____
   _____
   _____

8) Do you believe what you are pursuing is worth one more effort in spite of any obstacle, adversity, or negativity?
   _____
   _____

9) If you don't pursue it, what do you imagine the results would be?
   _____
   _____
   _____
   _____

10) What would it take or have to happen to remove this blockage?
    _____
    _____
    _____
    _____

11) What is at least 2 vital intangible assets that are needful in you moving pass this hinderance/blockage?
    _____
    _____
    _____

We don't have control over people thoughts, actions, behaviors, or what they try to label us as, but we do have power over our own.

12) Are you wearing labels that are destroying you? If so, what are they? They could have been put there by someone else or yourself.

_____
_____
_____
_____

I want you to think of one of your greatest desires that you want to happen. Now if someone told you that if you overcome/remove that label then I'll give you this desire. Would you say yes to it?

If you answered yes to this question, then your mind says it can be done. The label can be destroyed. You just need to take action.

Normally there is a reason why we fear rising and moving forward. We know that the possibility of better or greater is in our future, but there may be an underlying fear; such as, not having anyone but you to support you in the change and you don't know if you have what you need to support you – mentally & emotionally; who is going to encourage you; who is going to praise you for your actions or efforts.

13) What lack of support you sense may be an underlying fear that's holding you back, if any?

_____
_____
_____
_____
_____

The lepers were just sitting and waiting outside the gate for the circumstance to change, rather than rising to change it. They knew what things looked like behind them, but they didn't know what was before them. They only found out when they made a decision to rise up, change their position, and move froward to go and see. They had to know if what was before them pose a blessing or a curse, and they had to know before they met their fate – Death. They weren't for sure what they would find, but they knew it was better than waiting on death to find them.

Our going forward could make a difference. Moving forward holds the possibility or potential of change.

14) What can we do with what time we have left to set change in motion?

_____
_____
_____
_____

The lepers had no power to open the physical gate, but they had power to open the mind gate. They decided to open the gate of their mind, and made a decision to go forward. They put action to their decision and unlocked a gate into the miraculous. When they opened that gate and went forward, they entered into a whole new realm, because that is where God was waiting. God wasn't inside the gate Samaria, but famine and death were. He wasn't working miracles there. He was working a miracle among a selected few that said, "Let us rise and go"! When they did, they crossed the threshold into the miraculous!

We may not have certain resources to rise and change things, but we do have the power of mind and voice [meditation, affirmations, declaration/confessions of faith, and decrees].

15) There are many kinds of gates that keep us sitting next to the entrance, but never entering in. Just to name a few: fear, laziness, slumber, doubt, excuses, hinderance, various reasons, etc. There are some hindrances we can move, some we cannot. Is your gate really an hinderance or just an excuse for you not to make change?
_____
_____
_____

16) (a)Is there a gate God is waiting on you to decide to open or close? (b) What gate have you closed in? (c)What lies behind your locked gate? (d)What action do you need to take to close it?
_____
_____
_____
_____
_____

The lepers were rejected in the city, the gate was closed behind them, and they were sitting on the outside.

It hurts when we are rejected, but if we are not cautious it could become part of our mentality. And that in turn could do more damaged than the rejection (emotion) itself. It will cause a person to become closed in and afraid of trying because that thought of rejection will keep playing over and over in the mind. It will prevent a person from stepping out into new ventures.

17) Should we allow rejection and other things to cause us to sit till we die [dreams die, calling die, destiny never manifest, purpose never known nor fulfill, etc].
_____
_____

18) Does the weight of rejection, etc. outweighs your pursue of your dream?
_____
_____

19) How can you turn that around to the dream outweighing rejection, etc.?
_____
_____
_____
_____

Note:

The lepers didn't know that plenty awaited them in their near future. If they had accepted their position or condition as face value, they would have never known what was in store for them. When they rose up to move/go forward God rose up also. They rose up and started walking. At a certain point they saw provision. There was a trail before them. Hope rose up in them. They kept picking up provision until they enter the camp where there were an abundance supply.

God used them to fed/supply a whole nation. God directed them in the way they should go. There was a great wealth transfer initiated by the less likely.

God supernaturally drove the enemies from around or from guarding the wealth.

vv. 10 -17

The king had to have it verified/ confirmed what the lepers told them.
The Syrians left a trail of blessings of various kind. – v. 15

vv. 18 -20

The prophecy fulfilled.

Meditation Exercise:

Imagine that you are sitting outside a locked gate. For some reason someone locked you out. They rejected your presence and you are suddenly left alone. You sit there for sometime praying and crying out to God about your predicament. He brings to your remember a vision of success, a dream you forgot about, or a desire you wanted to fulfill. You sense He is saying to you, "Rise. Go and see." You rise. Going forward, and as you go you encounter a distinguish stranger who sense your despair. You tell him your situation. He says to you, "I will pray – Go and see!" You obey and keep walking. You walk for some distance and see a group of people camped near a river. They invite you to join them. They perceive that you are in a state of despair, but they inquire about your vision, dream, or desire. Upon you telling them, a female enters and says, "We need someone like you. We have been believing God to send us someone who can handle that kind of assignment. By faith we been gathering every thing they would need to start. What is your cost for helping us? Don't be shy about the figure. God has amply supplied our camp!" As you think about what you should ask, rejoice in the Lord for a while before opening your eyes.

∧∧

Students pray a prayer related to this miracle.

Date:_____
Session:_____

A Study of II Peter 1: 3 – 11
Growth In Christ:
An Entrance Into the Kingdom

¹ "Simon Peter, a servant and an apostle of Jesus Christ, to them that have obtained like precious faith with us through the righteousness of God and our Saviour Jesus Christ: ² Grace and peace be multiplied unto you through the knowledge of God, and of Jesus our Lord,"

V.3
An Abiding

"³ According as his divine power hath given unto us all things that pertain unto life and godliness, through the knowledge of him that hath called us to glory and virtue."

- (a) *..his divine power* [Jesus Our Lord] has granted to us [gifted to us] all things that pertain to an abundant life [personal; spiritual growth and maturity] and godliness [God's abiding nature],

Note: If God's nature is there, then so is His presence. We shouldn't be seeking a sensation/emotion experiences from the Lord, but we should be going after an "aboding" (Even the heart of God) that His abiding glory may remain within us and that we may walk continually in His abiding glory within. When we are faithful in <u>the abiding</u>, the glory will take us places in realms of the spirit and life.

"Jesus answered and said unto him, If a man love me, he will keep my words: and my Father will love him, and we will come unto him, and make our **abode** with him." John 14:23 KJB

The definition of *abode*-
a place of residence; a house or home. a stay; sojourn, dwelling, habitation.

"Let that therefore **abide** in you, which ye have heard from the beginning. If that which ye have heard from the beginning shall remain in you, ye also shall continue in the Son, and in the Father." I John 2:24 KJB

In "the abiding" is God or rather God is the abiding. God is love. Love activates power. It causes us to walk in power. A power that causes us to stand strong.

God wanted to reveal something to me. He had me separate abode to look like this [a-bode (a body)]
Then He said, " I'll make your house (body) my body."

How does your house/body become His body?
_____
_____
_____
_____

- (b) ...*through the knowledge of Him* [learning and taking in the knowledge of His word and the knowledge of Him (knowing Him)]. We can know Him through His nature.

(Not just taking in knowledge of His word, but getting to know Him and increasing in who He is or He increasing in us. Getting to know His nature is getting to know Him. When we know His nature, He expect
us to go after it to have it embedded in us. When we take on His nature, we see more of Him in us. With His nature in us, a governing body of kingdom principles govern us within.)

- (c) ...*called us to His own glory and virtue/excellence*. [Called us to be partaker of His own glory and holiness. To be transformed into His image is to put on Christ Jesus. The scriptures say from "glory to glory". Jesus prayed in John 17:20-26 that we make be one. He in us and we in Him. One new man!]

"But ye are a chosen generation, a royal priesthood, an holy nation, a peculiar people; that ye should shew forth the praises (virtue) of him who hath called you out of darkness into his marvellous light:" 1 Peter 2:9 KJB

The word "praises" translates to "virtue"

Virtue befits holiness.
befits – be appropriate for; suit. In keeping with. Fitting.

Define
virtue:_____
_____
_____

V.4
⁴ "Whereby are given unto us exceeding great and precious promises: that by these ye might be partakers of the divine nature, having escaped the corruption that is in the world through lust."

- (a) ....*exceeding great and precious promises* (by faith)
- Christ returning to reward the righteous
- To him that overcome.. See Rev. 2:7,11, 17,26-28; 3:5,12,21
- A new Heaven and a new Earth

- (b) .....*that by these*
- "all things that pertain unto life and godliness [that is written in His Word]
  He have given us in His word what we need to know how to live a whole life: spirit, mind, soul, body, relationship, and finances.

- (c) ....*ye might be partakers (become) of the divine nature*
- To an unspecific degree of His nature while on Earth
- The working of the Holy Spirit within
- God's divine nature infused in us in knowledge, holiness, righteousness (Matthew Poole's Commentary)

- His nature is expressed in the fruit of the Spirit – Gal. 5:22,23

(d) *....having escaped [being freed from bondage from] the corruption [degeneration] that is in the world in lust.*
- Corruption is rooted in lust

V. 5, 6, & 7

Our relationship with God is a personal one, but it is also a relationship of faith in who He say He is and can do what He says He can do. We cannot define a relationship with Him without adding to our faith. Peter tells us what to add to our relationship with God that these may reflect God to God in you and to man. He starts with adding virtue.

1) What is virtue?
   _____
   _____
   _____

2) What is Peter referring to when He tells us to add knowledge?
   _____
   _____
   _____

3) Define self-control and why it is important in everyday life?
   _____
   _____
   _____
   _____
   _____
   _____

4) What is steadfastness and why is it necessary that we maintain it?
   _____
   _____
   _____
   _____

5) How does the Bible define godliness or what is the Biblical standard of godliness?
   _____
   _____
   _____
   _____

6) How do you describe brotherly affection or what does brotherly affection looks (picture) like to you?
   _____
   _____
   _____
   _____

7) Love in this list is listed as last, but in all actually it is the top, for God is love.
   Is love more than an emotion? _____
   What is true love? _____
   _____

8) There are 7 sins in Prov. 6:16-19 that the Lord hates and are a reflection upon our character. How did the Lord say we show love to Him?

_____
_____
_____

9) How are some ways we can show character love to one another?

_____
_____
_____
_____

10) (a) Does it hurt sometimes to show the kind of love the Lord says we should show? Like "love those who hate you. Give them water when they are thirsty or food when they are hungry or turn the other cheek"? (b) What is God's objective (goal) in having us to response this way?

_____
_____
_____

V.8

8 "For if these things be in you [are your and become your nature] and abound [are increasing and transforming you], they make you that ye shall neither be barren nor unfruitful in the knowledge of our Lord Jesus Christ [the knowledge of His word and the knowledge of Him]."

These qualities advance a Christian in the knowledge of Jesus and the kingdom. They carry a heavy weight of honor and glory in the kingdom. They are access to greater kingdom treasures and blessings.

Quote: Those who are the most like Christ in their lives have the fullest knowledge of Him in this world, a knowledge to be perfected in the next world, when, purified from sin, "We shall see Him as He is." Ellicott's Commentary

V.9

9"But he that lacketh these things is blind, and cannot see afar off, and hath forgotten that he was purged from his old sins."

When we lack these qualities, we are blind and does not know what God/Jesus looks like. The Lord will not show himself in ways that we desire Him to. If He shows Himself, we cannot see Him or recognize Him. If He is moving or working around us, we won't perceive Him working.

V.10

10"Wherefore the rather, brethren, give diligence [of the upmost priority] to make your calling and election [relationship with God] sure: for if ye do these things [practice/ put in operation], ye shall never fall:"

Define *diligence:*

_____
_____

V. 11

¹¹"For so an entrance [access] shall be <u>ministered (given to you) unto you abundantly</u> into the everlasting kingdom of our Lord and Saviour Jesus Christ." King James Bible

¹¹"Then God will give you a grand entrance into the eternal Kingdom of our Lord and Savior Jesus Christ." New Living Translation

There is a connection between these qualities and us entering into the kingdom - **NOW,** and at our departure. As I said before, 'These qualities carry a heavy weight of glory (anointing, a covering) in the kingdom. They are access to realms.

(a)..an entrance/access – the gates will swing open or be open wide to you. Whatever gates that were closed, will open for you. Whatever gate a demon was guarding, will be destroyed. Angels will escort you into places and assist in the realm that you are in.

(b)...ministered to you abundantly – These qualities attract and employ an abundant of help/ service from angels. In Hebrews 1:1 it is said about angels, *"Are they not all ministering (serving) spirits, sent forth to minister for them who shall be heirs of salvation?"* Angels serve us.

It will be like God told Cyrus – Is. 45:1-3 *¹ "Thus saith the LORD to his anointed, to Cyrus, whose right hand I have holden, to subdue nations before him; and I will loose the loins of kings, to open before him the two leaved gates; and the gates shall not be shut; ²I will go before thee, and make the crooked places straight: I will break in pieces the gates of brass, and cut in sunder the bars of iron: ³And I will give thee the treasures of darkness, and hidden riches of secret places, that thou mayest know that I, the LORD, which call thee by thy name, am the God of Israel."*

- v.1 - He will strip evil powers and principalities of their powers that the gates will be opened and never shut again by them.
- v.2 - Whatever obstacles that God needs to remove, He will move to advance His kingdom in you and through you. Barriers will be destroyed and walls will fall. Where you had no favor, favor will start being seen. Area/s where you had no influence it will be granted.
- v.3 – You will start seeing resources provided. A kingdom door of resources will be opened to advance the kingdom (God's business) on Earth.

God wants to bring you into a large area so you can move around in the kingdom without restraints. He wants to bestow upon you, your inheritance as a child. An inheritance says, " I have enough that I don't have to look to the outside for help cause I'm connected! The Earth is mines and the fulness thereof!

****

Remember These Things

12 "Wherefore I will not be negligent to put you always in remembrance of these things, though ye know them, and be established in the present truth. 13Yea, I think it meet, as long as I am in this tabernacle, to stir you up by putting you in remembrance; 14Knowing that shortly I must put off this my tabernacle, even as our Lord Jesus Christ hath shewed me. 15Moreover I will endeavour that ye may be able after my decease to have these things always in remembrance."

****

Some Groundwork Information on Prayer
The Lord's instructions about prayer
(We can use this as a primer, especially when we can't seem to pray at times, or need help starting our prayer.)

⁵"And when you pray, you must not be like the hypocrites. For they love to stand and pray in the synagogues and at the street corners, that they may be seen by others. Truly, I say to you, they have received their reward. ⁶But when you pray, go into your room and shut the door and pray to your Father who is in secret. And your Father who sees in secret will reward you. ⁷"And when you pray, do not heap up empty phrases as the Gentiles do, for they think that they will be heard for their many words. ⁸Do not be like them, for your Father knows what you need before you ask him. ⁹Pray then like this:

The Lord's Prayer [Matt. 6:5 -15]

"Our Father in heaven, hallowed be your name. ¹⁰Your kingdom come, your will be done, on earth as it is in heaven. ¹¹Give us this day our daily bread, ¹²and forgive us our debts, as we also have forgiven our debtors. ¹³And lead us not into temptation, but deliver us from evil.

****

¹⁴For if you forgive others their trespasses, your heavenly Father will also forgive you, ¹⁵but if you do not forgive others their trespasses, neither will your Father forgive your trespasses.

The Lord's Prayer [Luke 11:2 - 4]

¹Now Jesus was praying in a certain place, and when he finished, one of his disciples said to him, "Lord, teach us to pray, as John taught his disciples." ²And he said to them, "When you pray, say: "Father, hallowed be your name. Your kingdom come. ³Give us each day our daily bread, ⁴and forgive us our sins, for we ourselves forgive everyone who is indebted to us. And lead us not into temptation"

We pray in Jesus' name. "Whatever you ask in My name, that will I do, so that the Father may be glorified in the Son. If you ask Me anything in My name, I will do it. " John 14:13-14

****

Tips for productive prayers:
- Line prayer up with the Word.
- Find out God's will and pray it.

There are works that promotes prayer:
- Reading the Word
- Praying
- Fasting
- Faith

As you grow in the Word, you will see that your prayers increase and changes.

The Word & Prayer

Col. 3:16 Tell us, *"Let the Word of Christ dwell in you richly in all wisdom;.."* If the Living Word of God dwell in us richly, then we will be spiritual rich in all things (love, joy, peace, prayer, life, etc.)

When you get filled with the Word, you can't help but to pray it out. The Word is our communication power.

The Word of God is important in prayer, because when we read the Word the radiant virtue of God flows in us. It fuels our spirit man, so we won't run out of life; liken to a car running out of gas. We got to keep fuel in it, if we want to keep traveling or going places.

The Word illuminates our spirit man/mind. Remember the Word is alive and active -- **Hebrews 4:12** and **John 6:63** *"It is the Spirit who gives life; the words that I speak unto you, they are spirit, and they are life."*

Prayer is communication with God. When we read the Word, a form of communication takes place. When we read the Word, God is looking at our face with a radiant life and that life reflects in our face to see Him as we read. So, when we read the Word, we come face to face with God/Jesus. We look at His face and read it and He at ours - Imparting blessings.

When you go up in levels of prayer, just remember what you did to get there is what you need to do to stay there. Stay consistent (unchangeable in godly nature).

Prayers are work, but they are also "labors of love".

Don't get lost in the work and neglect the love relationship. Just take some time to just "love on Jesus".

We may pray many prayers in faith, but nothing touches the heart of God greater than the prayers deep from the soul (soul-cry).   ["But the tax collector stood at a distance, He would not ever look up to heaven, but beat his breast and said, "God, have mercy on me, a sinner." Luke 18:13]

The Similar Between Jabez Prayer and The Lord's Prayer

And Jabez called on the God of Israel.
> Matt. 6:9 …Our Father which art in heaven, Hallowed be thy name.
>> 10^a Thy kingdom come.

Saying, oh that thou wouldest bless me indeed; and enlarge my coast;
> Matt. 6:10^b …Thy will be done in earth, as it is in heaven. "Give us this day our daily bread."
>> Your kingdom have the authority and power to do this, to make it happen.

And that thine hand might be with me,
> Matt. 6:12 "And forgive us our trespasses, as we forgive those who trespass against us.
>> To show mercy and forgiveness

And that thou wouldest keep me from evil.
> Matt. 6:13 "And lead us not into temptation, but deliver us from the evil (evil one)

For thine is the kingdom, and the power, and the glory, for ever. Amen
> Acknowledging that God controls it all.

SEEING OR REVEALING ME (List)

[GROWING IN CHRIST: CHARACTER BUILDING]
Gal. 5:22-24; Col. 3:12; 2 Peter1:5-8

- Bible Character to do evaluation on (chosen by Teacher/Mentor)
  [Characters: Adam, Eve, Cain, Abel, Noah, Abraham, Sarah, Jacob, Esau, Hagar, etc]

  *There are several Lists of Values, Characters, Attributes, Strengths & Weaknesses that came with <u>Welcome Package</u>, you can use the lists to help identify values, characters, attributes, strengths & weaknesses of the chosen character.

Note: You can use the chart or notebook paper, if you need more space to answer the questions.

1. Character
   _____

2. What Virtue, Character, Value, or Attribute from *Lists you saw in this character?

   _____
   _____
   _____

3. What is the opposite/s or negative that you saw?

   _____
   _____
   _____

4. Did you see yourself in this person? Explain.

   _____
   _____
   _____

5. If it was the opposite, what action/s can you take to make it praiseworthy?

   _____
   _____
   _____

MENTOR'S SPEECH
By Barbara A. Perry

Good day Mentees!

We have come to the conclusion of the mentoring and coaching sessions.

1st Stanza or Segment

In our sessions --

We have watched Jesus miraculously turn water into wine.

We have experienced Moses releasing phenomenal miracles and Aaron performing the supernatural.

We have felt the despair of Peter and his partner and how Jesus intervened at a point of need.

We have witnessed the mercy and compassion shown by Jesus as He liberated 2 castaways, schizophrenia, despondence, demon-possessed men.

We have watched and observed Naaman the leper, and how pride and the frustration of others' action brought him to the point where he almost missed his miracle.

We have saw through the eyes of the widow the phenomenal benefits of faithful service in the kingdom.

We have walked in the steps of the lepers, only to find that God was waiting along the way to bless us to success.

2nd Stanza or Segment

From the water to wine, we tasted change.

Through the miracles we saw hope for change.

From the despair we saw a need supplied.

From a state of no return, we saw mercy, compassion, liberation, and life restored.

Through the increase of the widow's oil, we saw that GOD'S WELL does not run dry for the faithful.

Through the rising up and going forth of the 4 lepers we have saw the results of never giving up, that there is hope for our tomorrow.

****

So, as we conclude these sessions may we continue to journey by faith, guided by a light that never grows dim. Let us not sit still till we die. But let us forever strive to find and take hold of our success, as those who seek their fortune at the end of a rainbow. Though theirs may be an empty promise, ours is not. For ours is by covenant!

May God continually richly bless you and prosper all your endeavors, in Christ Jesus!

End of the Class Survey & Personal Evaluation Questions

1. What is your view about this class/session?

   _____
   _____
   _____
   _____
   _____

2. Would you recommend it to someone else?

   _____
   _____
   _____

3. What would you say needs to be improved on in these sessions?

   _____
   _____
   _____
   _____

4. Do you believe you have gained something from these sessions that you didn't have before? If so, what?

   _____
   _____
   _____
   _____

5. Other than spiritual knowledge, what have you gained personally?

   _____
   _____
   _____
   _____

6. What do you perceive have changed in you personally through these sessions?

   _____
   _____
   _____
   _____

7. Do you feel you have a clearer view of your calling, purpose, or capability to serve in some form? or are you assured of your reason for existing?

   _____
   _____
   _____
   _____

8. Do you believe in yourself that you can be a leader to some degree?

9. Do you have confidence in the Holy Spirit within you to help you in whatever assignment He gives you, or guide you in whatever you put your hands to do for the kingdom?

10. If you were supplied with the material used in these sessions, would you feel confidence to hold sessions?

11. Can you express yourself easier in talking or writing?

12. Would you feel confident in putting together a class lesson after viewing the lessons you took part in?

13. Do you believe you are a good problem solver?

14. Do you believe that problem solvers have all the answers?

15. Are you more of a talker than a listener?

16. Is it more important to be a listener or a talker?

17. James 1:19 tells us to be swift to hear, slow to speak. Why is it more important to be a listener?

18. Do you believe you listen well enough to counsel someone?

19. Is it okay to share our views/opinions, tell someone what we would do, or what someone else did; if we don't have the answers, they are seeking help/advise on?

    _____
    _____
    _____

20. If you want to know something or discover something, what should you ask?

    _____
    _____

21. Do you hear only what is said, or hear more than what is being said?

    For instance: If John came and told you that someone stole his dog and he blamed Ken, what information did John leave out that you need to know, before talking with Ken?

    _____
    _____
    _____

**Please sign & return to
Leader/Teacher/Mentor/Coach**_____

NOTES

ABOUT THE AUTHOR

Barbara A. Perry is a servant and apostle of the Lord. She has been ministering the Word for over 30 years. She is a Christian author and sole proprietor of Garden 33 Publisher – An independent book ministry. She has two daughters: Alice and Samantha and four grandchildren: Da'Shawn, Samara, Natalie, and Harmonie.

Other books by Barbara A. Perry:

We Are Gods companion to
   Faith & The Celestial Kingdom

Release The Greatness That's Within You

PIAS: Supernatural Sessions

The Blessing of Numbers 6:22 –27

Treasures From The Word

Website: barbaraperry.wixsite.com/garden-33-publisher

Email: elohimestatemlc@yahoo.com

Website for **Downloads**:
barbaraperry.wixsite.com/elohimestatemlc

www.ingramcontent.com/pod-product-compliance
Lightning Source LLC
Chambersburg PA
CBHW081330190426
43193CB00044B/2905